Wonder Blocks
Stack, Cut, Sew, and Go

TERRY MARTIN

Martingale®
& COMPANY

Wonder Blocks: Stack, Cut, Sew, and Go
© 2008 by Terry Martin

Martingale® & COMPANY

That Patchwork Place® is an imprint of Martingale & Company®.

Martingale & Company
20205 144th Ave. NE
Woodinville, WA 98072-8478 USA
www.martingale-pub.com

Printed in China
13 12 11 10 09 08   8 7 6 5 4 3 2 1

Library of Congress Cataloging-in-Publication Data
Library of Congress Control Number: 2007041246

ISBN: 978-1-56477-771-3

Credits

President & CEO • *Tom Wierzbicki*
Publisher • *Jane Hamada*
Editorial Director • *Mary V. Green*
Managing Editor • *Tina Cook*
Technical Editor • *Laurie Baker*
Copy Editor • *Sheila Chapman Ryan*
Design Director • *Stan Green*
Assistant Design Director • *Regina Girard*
Illustrator • *Adrienne Smitke*
Cover & Text Designer • *Adrienne Smitke*
Photographer • *Brent Kane*

Mission Statement

Dedicated to providing quality products and service to inspire creativity.

◆

Dedication

To everyone who loves the simple joys of life: family, friends, and a quick and easy quilt pattern!

Contents

Introduction ◆ 5

Wonder Block Construction ◆ 6

The Projects

Safe Harbor ◆ 9

Batik Blast ◆ 12

Gold Rush ◆ 15

Home at Last ◆ 19

About the Author ◆ 24

Busy Bee Quilt Guild Raffle Quilt, 2004, 101" x 101".
Designed by Terry Martin. Quilted by Barbara Dau. Darlene Larsen won the raffle quilt and is the owner!

Introduction

I joined the Busy Bee quilt guild of Snohomish, Washington, several years ago. In the guild I have created blocks for fellow guild members and done other bits of volunteer quilting here and there, but I generally keep a low profile. In 2004, the guild president at the time, Barb Dau, who is also one of my favorite professional machine quilters, gave me a call one evening. "Terry," she said, "I'm looking for someone to head the raffle-quilt committee this year, and I know it's late notice, but I want you to do it." My first thought was *YIKES! That's a lot of work!* My practical side urged me to politely say I couldn't squeeze it into my schedule. However, my creative mind betrayed me, and I instantly started thinking of a design. Before I could take it back I heard myself saying, "Gosh, I'm flattered that you would ask me and I would love to do it." Was that me saying those words?

The time frame for the raffle quilt was short; we were already a couple of months behind schedule. The quilt criteria was this: it had to be striking so people would buy lots of tickets; it had to fit a standard bed (it came out king-size); it had to be done fast; it had to be easy enough that brand-new quilters could help make blocks; it had to include appliqué (not my forte); and finally, the blocks all had to be the same size so sewing them together would be flawless. Needless to say, I had my work cut out for me.

Wonder blocks to the rescue! I had been toying with the idea of creating super-simple 6" blocks that, when put together in a random fashion, create an allover effect with very little seam matching required. As a matter of fact, with Wonder blocks it's nearly impossible to create any particular pattern, either in the block positioning or fabric selection. So, with seven different simply designed blocks, fabulous batik fabrics, and the help of Darlene Larsen, appliquér extraordinaire from the guild, the raffle quilt came together quickly and easily. Barb Dau added the finishing touch with fabulous machine quilting.

But I couldn't stop thinking about all the different applications these fun, easy, and simple blocks could lend themselves to—thus, this book. Be careful—the super easy cutting and piecing instructions will hook you and you'll want to make several of these fun quilts.

There are many possible configurations of the Wonder block, and they are easy and fun to assemble.

Fabric Selection and Preparation

The first thing you'll need to do is to select your fabrics. Most of the projects in this book use between six and eight different fabrics. If you look at the project photos, you'll see that the fabrics are cut into different-sized pieces and mixed up throughout the quilt, which makes it easy to select fabrics because none is really taking the spotlight. In essence, if your fabrics work together well on the bolt or in a group of fat quarters, they'll look fabulous together in the quilt.

Under most circumstances I don't prewash my fabrics and I'm suggesting you don't either, especially for projects that use fat quarters. For some of the projects using fat quarters, the fat quarter will need to measure no less than 18" x 22", and you are going to use every thread to make the blocks. If you prewash your fabrics, use a larger piece to begin with, or cut an 18" x 22" piece from a larger prewashed piece of fabric.

Don't be discouraged if your fat quarters or fabric pieces aren't big enough. You have options! If you just *have* to use the fat quarters that aren't up to size (and believe me I know from experience!), simply make fewer blocks and a smaller quilt, or you could make smaller-sized blocks. You will be able to use every bit of your fabric and still have a striking quilt.

The Wonder Pieces

There are seven different Wonder blocks used in this book, with each block made up of a different combination or configuration of square and rectangular shapes labeled A–F. Each quilt uses all seven blocks. If you play with the shapes long enough, you'll realize that there are many more Wonder blocks that can be made from these six pieces.

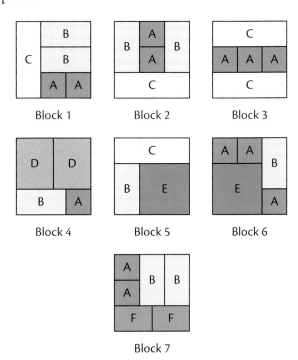

Block 1   Block 2   Block 3

Block 4   Block 5   Block 6

Block 7

My original seven blocks were designed to finish at 6" square. Once I had the cutting and piecing down for those blocks, it was easy to see how the block pieces could be resized to make smaller and larger blocks. The chart on page 7 will give you the dimensions to cut each shape to make blocks ranging from 3" to 12". The number of pieces of each shape to cut to make one of each of the seven blocks is also given.

Basic Cutting for Wonder Blocks

Select the size of block you want to make; then cut the number of pieces required for each shape of that size. The cutting sequence for each of the projects is detailed in the project instructions.

Piece	Number to Cut	3" Block	4½" Block	6" Block	9" Block	12" Block
A	13	1½" x 1½"	2" x 2"	2½" x 2½"	3½" x 3½"	4½" x 4½"
B	9	1½" x 2½"	2" x 3½"	2½" x 4½"	3½" x 6½"	4½" x 8½"
C	5	1½" x 3½"	2" x 5"	2½" x 6½"	3½" x 9½"	4½" x 12½"
D	2	2" x 2½"	2¾" x 3½"	3½" x 4½"	5" x 6½"	6½" x 8½"
E	2	2½" x 2½"	3½" x 3½"	4½" x 4½"	6½" x 6½"	8½" x 8½"
F	2	1½" x 2"	2" x 2¾"	2½" x 3½"	3½" x 5"	4½" x 6½"

For blocks that are 6" or smaller, you can cut all the pieces you need to create 56 blocks from eight fat quarters. And because you are cutting the exact same pieces from each fat quarter, you can stack the fabrics and cut them all at once. How easy is that? As you cut each piece, make stacks for each shape. This will make the piecing process much easier.

Putting the Pieces Together

Place the stacks of cut pieces next to your sewing machine in alphabetical order. If you stacked and cut your fabrics together, the fabrics will be in random order, which is what you want. If you cut all of the same shape from one fabric at a time, you might want to mix up the stacks to create more of a random order when piecing. The piecing methods I give you will also help create a truly scrappy look, so don't obsess over this too much. It's OK if two pieces cut from the same fabric end up next to each other.

The piecing sequence for each of the seven blocks is shown on page 8. I recommend that you make a copy of this to keep next to your machine as you are making your blocks. Then select one of the piecing methods on page 8 to ensure that you have a true scrappy look. I have used each of them and they work equally well. Try them out and discover your favorite method, or create your own system.

I also recommend that wherever possible you chain piece the pieces together. Sew the first pair of pieces from cut edge to cut edge. At the end of the seam, stop sewing, but don't cut the thread. Feed the next pair of pieces under the presser foot, as close as possible to the first pair. Continue feeding pieces through the machine without cutting the thread in between. When all the pieces have been sewn, remove the chain from the machine, clip the threads between the units, and press the seam allowances.

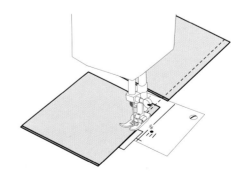

Method One. Using chain piecing, sew together all of the pieces for one of the block variations. For example, if you are piecing block 1, sew all the A pieces together in pairs and all the B pieces together in pairs. Cut the threads between the pairs to separate them, and then chain piece a B pair to each A pair. Cut those units apart and chain piece a C piece to each unit to complete the blocks. Make sure you randomly choose the fabric segments when sewing them together to create a scrappy look.

Method Two. Using chain piecing, sew together the first sequence of pieces from each of the seven different block variations. Cut them apart and put them in stacks labeled 1–7 to correspond with the block number. Continue sewing the first sequence of pieces together until you have the amount needed to make the necessary blocks. Sew the second sequence from each of the seven blocks together in the same

manner and so forth until all of the seven blocks are complete. This method automatically creates a scrappy look, but you have to be careful when restacking the sewn segments so that each sequence is in the correct stack for that block number.

Method Three. Several of the blocks contain the same pieced units. For example, the A square is sewn together in pairs in four of the seven different block variations. For this method, sew the same pieced units together at one time using chain piecing. (The project instructions will tell you how many of each block to make so you can determine the number of units to make.) Next, find another common pieced unit and sew them all together. After you have a stack of each of the units, sew them together with the other necessary pieces to complete the block.

Piecing Sequence for Wonder Blocks

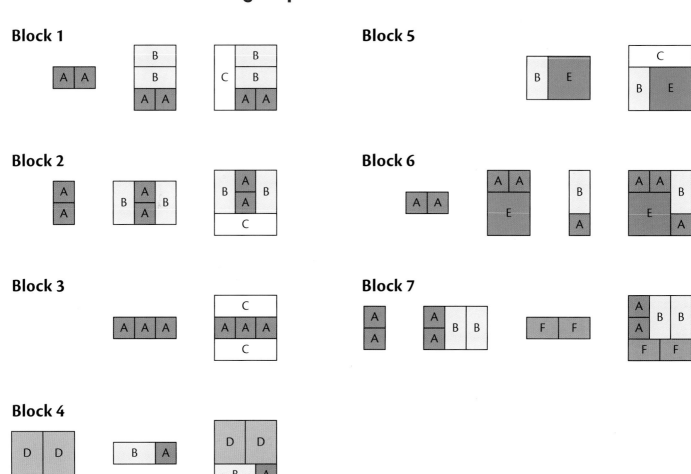

Safe Harbor

I love batiks, and this batik panel was originally purchased to be the back of a kimono jacket. Now I can enjoy seeing it on a wall instead of on my back!

Start with a fabric panel, surround it with Wonder blocks, and in no time flat you'll have a wall hanging or table topper! I love working with a black, red, and white color theme because it creates a dramatic look with bold contrast (and it worked perfectly with the panel I selected), but you easily can substitute colors that coordinate with your panel choice.

Finished Quilt: 36" x 40½"
Finished Blocks: 4½" x 4½"

Materials

All yardages are based on 42"-wide fabric unless otherwise noted.

18½" x 23" Asian scene batik panel for quilt center
8 fat quarters of assorted red, black, and white
    prints for blocks
⅜ yard of black print for binding
1⅜ yards of fabric for backing
42" x 46" piece of batting

Coping with Panels

If you want to use a novelty fabric panel that's not quite as large as the size called for here, you can simply add coping strips to one or more sides of the panel. Coping strips are essentially borders around the panel used to bring the panel up to the necessary size. The Asian panel I used for this quilt was a little smaller than I needed to fit my blocks, so I added coping strips on all four sides. You could also offset the panel by adding the coping strips to only one side and the bottom, producing a look that's similar to an Attic Window block.

Cutting

Stack the fat quarters together, right sides up, and cut them all at once for fast and easy cutting. All measurements include ¼"-wide seam allowances.

From *each* of the 8 fat quarters, cut:
1 strip, 3½" x 22"; crosscut into:
    2 squares, 3½" x 3½" (E)
    2 rectangles, 2¾" x 3½" (D)
    3 rectangles, 2" x 3½" (B)
4 strips, 2" x 22"; crosscut:
    1 strip into 4 rectangles, 2" x 5" (C)
    1 strip into:
        1 rectangle, 2" x 5" (C)
        4 rectangles, 2" x 3½" (B)
    1 strip into:
        2 rectangles, 2" x 3½" (B)
        2 rectangles, 2" x 2¾" (F)
        3 squares, 2" x 2" (A)
    1 strip into 10 squares, 2" x 2" (A)

From the binding print, cut:
4 strips, 2½" x 42"

Making the Blocks

1. Stack each of the same-shaped units together and place the groups in alphabetical order next to your sewing machine. Place the piecing sequence for each of the seven blocks (page 8) next to your sewing machine also.
2. Choose your favorite piecing method (page 8) and stitch the blocks together. Make eight of each of the seven different Wonder blocks (56 total).

Assembling the Quilt Top

1. Randomly select two blocks and sew them together. Repeat to make a total of 26 pairs. Set aside the remaining four blocks for another project.
2. Sew five pairs together side by side to make a side border. Make two.

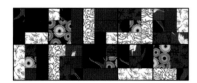

Make 2.

3. Sew the side borders to the sides of the center panel. Press the seam allowances toward the borders.

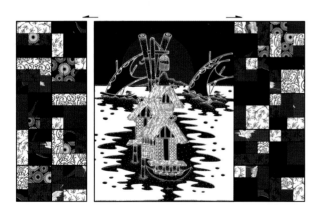

4. Sew eight of the remaining pairs together side by side to make the top border. Repeat to make the bottom border.

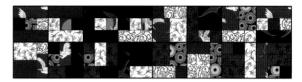

Make 2.

5. Sew the top and bottom borders to the center panel. Press the seam allowances toward the borders.

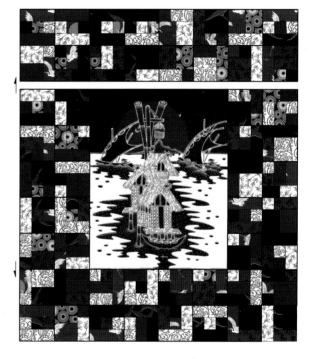

Finishing the Quilt

1. Layer the quilt top with batting and backing. Baste the layers together.
2. Hand or machine quilt as desired.
3. Square up the quilt sandwich.
4. Prepare and sew the binding to the quilt. Add a hanging sleeve, if desired, and a label.

Batik Blast

I asked Becky Marshall to machine quilt this sunny quilt. Her long-arm machine quilting has a wonderfully whimsical look, and she has added the perfect touch!

Setting the Wonder blocks on point adds even more interest, especially when you use bright batiks! My friend Lorraine Jones owns an online quilt shop that features batiks and Asian-print fabrics. She brought some of her inventory to sell at our quilt guild's annual quilt show, and what fun I had shopping for this quilt! I knew I wanted something bright, and I found eight perfect single-colored batik fat quarters. *Excellent!* I thought to myself. I would worry about the rest of the fabric later. Then, while standing in line to pay for my goodies, a sunflower batik print was winking at me from across the booth. I have come to the conclusion that when a fabric winks at you, you need to buy at least 4 yards, so I did. The fabric was the perfect accompaniment to the fat quarters.

Finished Quilt: 67" x 75½"
Finished Blocks: 6" x 6"

Materials

All yardages are based on 42"-wide fabric unless otherwise noted.

3¾ yards of floral batik for blocks, setting triangles, borders, and binding
9 assorted fat quarters for blocks
4 yards of fabric for backing
72" x 80" piece of batting

Cutting

Stack the fat quarters together, right sides up, and cut them all at once for fast and easy cutting. All measurements include ¼"-wide seam allowances.

From *each* of the 9 fat quarters, cut:
7 strips, 2½" x 22"; crosscut:
    5 strips *each* into:
        1 rectangle, 2½" x 6½" (C)
        2 rectangles, 2½" x 4½" (B)
        2 squares, 2½" x 2½" (A)
    1 strip into:
        1 rectangle, 2½" x 6½" (C)
        1 rectangle, 2½" x 4½" (B)
        3 squares, 2½" x 2½" (A)
    1 strip into:
        3 rectangles, 2½" x 3½" (F)
        3 squares, 2½" x 2½" (A)

From the floral batik, cut:
5 strips, 4½" x 42"; crosscut:
    2 strips *each* into 9 squares, 4½" x 4½" (E)
    1 strip into 11 rectangles, 3½" x 4½" (D)
    1 strip into:
        4 squares, 4½" x 4½" (E)
        6 rectangles, 3½" x 4½" (D)
    1 strip into 5 rectangles, 3½" x 4½" (D). From the remainder of the strip, cut 1 rectangle, 2½" x 6½" (C).
2 strips, 9¾" x 42"; crosscut into 6 squares, 9¾" x 9¾"; cut each square twice diagonally to yield 24 triangles (you will use only 22 triangles). From the remainder of the leftover strip, cut 2 squares, 5⅛" x 5⅛"; cut each square once diagonally to yield 4 triangles.
7 strips, 8½" x 42"
8 binding strips, 2½" x 42"

Making the Blocks

1. Stack each of the same-shaped units together and place the groups in alphabetical order next to your sewing machine. Place the piecing sequence for each of the seven blocks (page 8) next to your sewing machine.
2. Choose your favorite piecing method (page 8) and stitch the blocks together. Make 11 of each of the 7 different Wonder blocks (77 total). You will have one extra A piece and five extra F pieces.

Assembling the Quilt Top

1. Refer to the quilt assembly diagram below to arrange 72 blocks into diagonal rows. Rearrange the blocks until you are satisfied with the look of the quilt center. You will have five blocks left over.
2. Add the floral batik corner and side setting triangles to your arrangement.
3. Sew the blocks and triangles in each row together. Press the seam allowances in alternating directions from row to row. Sew the rows together, adding the corner triangles last.

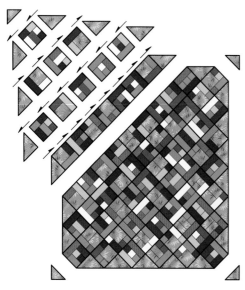

Quilt assembly

4. Join the floral batik 8½" x 42" strips end to end. Press the seam allowances to one side.
5. Measure the quilt through the center from top to bottom and cut two border strips to this measurement. Sew the borders to the sides of the quilt center. Press the seam allowances toward the borders.
6. Measure the quilt through the center from side to side, including the borders you just added. From the remainder of the pieced floral batik strip, cut two strips to this measurement. Sew the borders to the top and bottom of the quilt center. Press the seam allowances toward the borders.

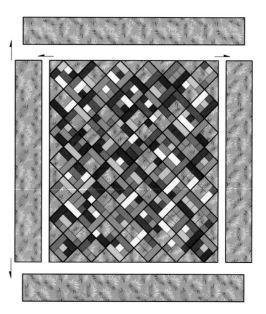

Finishing the Quilt

1. Layer the quilt top with batting and backing. Baste the layers together.
2. Hand or machine quilt as desired.
3. Square up the quilt sandwich.
4. Prepare and sew the binding to the quilt. Add a hanging sleeve, if desired, and a label.

Gold Rush

The muted batik prints with the gold ink spread across them present quite a contrast to "Batik Blast" on page 12. Rhoda Reynolds chose a straight setting with inner borders, 6" blocks for the body of the quilt, and 4½" blocks for the border.

When I was playing with Wonder blocks I became totally hooked, but I wondered what other quilters would think of this super fast and easy idea. So I asked several people if they wouldn't mind making their own Wonder block quilts. Ah, success. Their responses were all favorable, and one quilter in particular, Rhoda Reynolds, really embraced the concept. I'm not quite sure how many quilts she made using Wonder blocks, but this one is beautiful! All the batik fabrics she used were printed with a gold metallic shine on them. I wish you could see this quilt in person because it really glows!

Finished Quilt: 59½" x 66¼"
Finished Blocks: 6" x 6"
Finished Border Blocks: 4½" x 4½"

Materials

All yardages are based on 42"-wide fabric unless otherwise noted.

1⅓ yards of gold tone-on-tone print for outer border and binding
⅜ yard of gold striped fabric for inner border
8 fat quarters (each must measure at least 18" x 22") for center blocks
8 fat quarters for border blocks
3¾ yards of fabric for backing
66" x 72" piece of batting

Cutting

Stack the fat quarters together, right sides up, and cut them all at once for fast and easy cutting. Keep the pieces for the 6" center blocks separate from the 4½" border blocks to avoid confusion while piecing. All measurements include ¼"-wide seam allowances.

From *each* of the 8 fat quarters for center blocks, cut:

1 strip, 4½" x 18"; crosscut into:
    2 squares, 4½" x 4½" (E)
    2 rectangles, 3½" x 4½" (D)
7 strips, 2½" x 18"; crosscut:
    4 strips each into:
        1 rectangle, 2½" x 6½" (C)
        2 rectangles, 2½" x 4½" (B)

1 strip into:
    1 rectangle, 2½" x 6½" (C)
    1 rectangle, 2½" x 4½" (B)
    1 rectangle, 2½" x 3½" (F)
    1 square, 2½" x 2½" (A)
1 strip into:
    5 squares, 2½" x 2½" (A)
    1 rectangle, 2½" x 3½" (F)
1 strip into 7 squares, 2½" x 2½" (A)

From *each* of the 8 fat quarters for border blocks, cut:

1 strip, 3½" x 20"; crosscut into:
    2 squares, 3½" x 3½" (E)
    2 rectangles, 2¾" x 3½" (D)
    3 rectangles, 2" x 3½" (B)
4 strips, 2" x 20"; crosscut:
    1 strip into 4 rectangles, 2" x 5" (C)
    1 strip into 10 squares, 2" x 2" (A)
    1 strip into:
        1 rectangle, 2" x 5" (C)
        4 rectangles, 2" x 3½" (B)
    1 strip into:
        1 rectangles, 2" x 3½" (B)
        2 rectangles, 2" x 2¾" (F)
        2 squares, 2" x 2" (A)

From the gold striped fabric, cut:
5 strips, 2" x 42"

From the gold tone-on-tone print, cut:
7 strips, 3¼" x 42"
7 binding strips, 2½" x 42"

Making the Blocks

1. Stack each of the same-shaped units together for the 6" center blocks and place the groups in alphabetical order next to your sewing machine. Place the piecing sequence for each of the seven blocks (page 8) next to your sewing machine.
2. Choose your favorite piecing method (page 8) and stitch the blocks together. Make eight of each of the seven different Wonder blocks (56 total).
3. Repeat steps 1 and 2 with the pieces for the 4½" border blocks to make seven of each of the seven different Wonder blocks (49 total). You will have 5 extra A pieces, 1 extra B piece, 5 extra C pieces, and 2 extra D, E, and F pieces. Set aside two C pieces to use in the outer border.

Assembling the Quilt Top

1. Arrange the 6½" blocks into eight rows of seven blocks each. Rearrange the blocks until you are satisfied with the look of the quilt center.
2. Sew the blocks in each row together. Press the seam allowances in alternating directions from row to row.

Make 8.

3. Sew the rows together. Press the seam allowances in one direction.

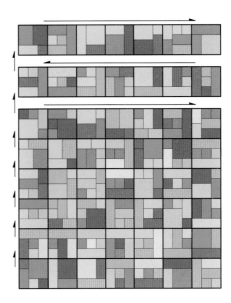

Adding the Borders

1. Join the 2" x 42" gold striped strips end to end to make one long strip. Press the seam allowances to one side. From the pieced strip, cut two inner-border strips, 2" x 48½". Sew the borders to the sides of the quilt center. Press the seam allowances toward the border strips. From the remainder of the pieced strip, cut two inner-border strips, 2" x 45½". Sew the borders to the top and bottom of the quilt center. Press the seam allowances toward the border strips.
2. Sew 11 of the 4½" blocks together end to end. Make two strips. Add a C piece to either end of each strip. Press the seam allowances in one direction. Sew these strips to the sides of the quilt top. Press the seam allowances toward the inner border.

Make 2.

3. Sew 12 of the 4½" blocks together end to end. Make two strips. (You will have eight blocks left over.) Press the seam allowances in one direction. Sew these strips to the top and bottom of the quilt top. Press the seam allowances toward the inner border.

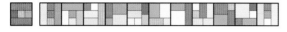

Make 2.

4. Join the 3¼" x 42" gold print strips end to end to make one long strip. Press the seam allowances to one side. Measure the quilt top through the center from top to bottom. From the pieced strip, cut two outer-border strips to the length measured. Sew the strips to the sides of the quilt top. Press the seam allowances toward the outer-border strips.

5. Measure the quilt top through the center from side to side, including the just-added borders. From the remainder of the pieced gold print strip, cut two outer border strips to the length measured. Sew the strips to the top and bottom of the quilt top. Press the seam allowances toward the outer-border strips.

Finishing the Quilt

1. Layer the quilt top with batting and backing. Baste the layers together.
2. Hand or machine quilt as desired.
3. Square up the quilt sandwich.
4. Prepare and sew the binding to the quilt. Add a hanging sleeve, if desired, and a label.

Home at Last

Purple, green, and yellow is a classic combination of color for a pretty quilt.
These orphaned blocks really pop when surrounded by Wonder blocks.

I bought the nine purple-and-yellow Iris blocks at my quilt guild's annual auction; they were so cute and I knew just what to do with them. Some were hand pieced, some had signatures written along a seam line, most were 9½" unfinished (you know how that goes), but they were all darling and needed to be in a quilt.

Tell me, how many orphan blocks do you have? Obviously at one time the blocks were wonderful, but somehow they were put aside for another day. Well, today's the day! Most orphan blocks I come across (and yes, I too have my share) are standard sizes and fit well with the Wonder block scheme. So check the cedar chest and the project box high on the shelf (you know, the one way in back), and let those blocks shine again, accented by Wonder blocks. If you don't have any orphan blocks, you can also use a panel print. Just fussy cut the desired motifs into 9½" squares. What can be more fun, fast, and easy? And if the orphan quilt needs a good home, a charity organization will love to put it into the arms of a happy recipient.

Finished Quilt: 63" x 63"
Finished Blocks: 9" x 9"

Materials

All yardages are based on 42"-wide fabric unless otherwise noted.

9 orphan blocks, 9½" x 9½" (materials and instructions for making the Iris blocks shown in the featured quilt are given on page 22)
⅔ yard *each* of six different purple, green, and yellow print fabrics for Wonder blocks*
⅝ yard of fabric for binding
4 yards of fabric for backing
70" x 70" piece of batting

*I used more than six fabrics for a scrappier look, but six fabrics are all you need to make the 40 blocks required for this project.

Cutting

Stack the Wonder block fabrics together, right sides up, and cut them all at once for fast and easy cutting. All measurements include ¼"-wide seam allowances.

From *each* of the 6 purple, green, and yellow prints, cut:
1 strip, 6½" x 42"; crosscut into:
    2 squares, 6½" x 6½" (E)
    2 rectangles, 5" x 6½" (D)
    4 rectangles, 3½" x 6½" (B)
4 strips, 3½" x 42"; crosscut:
    1 strip into:
        5 rectangles, 3½" x 6½" (B)
        2 squares, 3½" x 3½" (A)
    1 strip into 4 rectangles, 3½" x 9½" (C)
    1 strip into:
        1 rectangle, 3½" x 9½" (C)
        8 squares, 3½" x 3½" (A)
    1 strip into:
        3 squares, 3½" x 3½" (A)
        2 rectangles, 3½" x 5" (F)

From the binding fabric, cut:
7 strips, 2½" x 42"

Making the Wonder Blocks

1. Stack each of the same-shaped units together and place the groups in alphabetical order next to your sewing machine. Place the piecing sequence for each of the seven blocks (page 8) next to your sewing machine.
2. Choose your favorite piecing method (page 8) and stitch the blocks together. Make six of each of the seven different Wonder blocks (42 total).

Assembling the Quilt Top

1. Refer to the quilt assembly diagram below to arrange the Wonder blocks and orphan blocks into seven rows. Rearrange the Wonder blocks until you are satisfied with the look of the quilt center.

2. Sew the blocks in each row together. Press the seam allowances in alternating directions from row to row.
3. Sew the rows together. Press the seam allowances in one direction.

Finishing the Quilt

1. Layer the quilt top with batting and backing. Baste the layers together.
2. Hand or machine quilt as desired.
3. Square up the quilt sandwich.
4. Prepare and sew the binding to the quilt. Add a hanging sleeve, if desired, and a label.

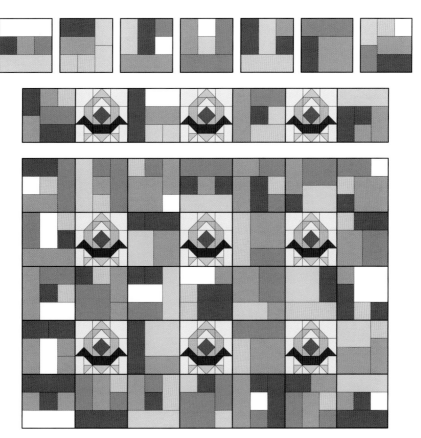

Quilt assembly

Iris Block

If you don't have any orphan blocks or if you want to re-create the featured quilt, follow the instructions below to create nine Iris blocks.

Materials

1¼ yards *total* of assorted yellow print scraps
⅜ yard *total* of assorted purple print scraps
⅓ yard *total* of assorted dark green print scraps
¼ yard *total* of assorted light green print scraps
⅛ yard *total* of assorted magenta print scraps

Cutting (for one block)

Repeat these instructions nine times. Keep the pieces for each block together to make piecing easier. All measurements include ¼"-wide seam allowances.

From one yellow print, cut:
2 squares, 3½" x 3½"
5 squares, 2⅜" x 2⅜"; cut each square once
    diagonally to yield 10 triangles
4 rectangles, 2" x 3½"
1 square, 4¼" x 4¼"; cut twice diagonally to yield
    4 triangles. You will use only 1 of the triangles.

From one purple print, cut:
2 rectangles, 2" x 3½"
2 squares, 2" x 2"
2 squares, 2⅜" x 2⅜"; cut each square once
    diagonally to yield 4 triangles

From one magenta print, cut:
1 square, 2⅝" x 2⅝"

From one dark green print, cut:
4 squares, 2" x 2"
1 square, 2⅜" x 2⅜"; cut once diagonally to yield
    2 triangles
1 rectangle, 2" x 3½"

From one light green print, cut:
1 square, 4¼" x 4¼"; cut twice diagonally to yield
    4 triangles. You will use only 2 of the triangles.
1 square, 2⅜" x 2⅜"; cut once diagonally to yield
    2 triangles

Making the Iris Blocks

1. Sew two yellow and two purple 2⅜" triangles to the sides of the magenta square as shown. Press the seam allowances toward the triangles.

Make 1.

2. Sew yellow 2⅜" triangles to the short sides of a light green 4¼" triangle. Make two. Sew purple 2⅜" triangles to the short sides of a yellow 4¼" triangle. Make one. Press the seam allowances toward the small triangles.

Make 2.   Make 1.

3. Sew the units created in steps 1 and 2 and the dark green rectangle together as shown. Press the seam allowances away from the center unit.

4. Draw a line from corner to corner on the wrong side of the purple 2" squares. With right sides together, lay a marked square in the corner of a yellow 3½" square as shown. Sew on the marked line. Trim ¼" from the stitched line. Press the purple triangle toward the corner of the yellow square. Make two.

Make 2.

5. Draw a line from corner to corner on the wrong side of the dark green 2" squares. With right sides together, lay a marked square in the lower-right corner of a yellow and a purple rectangle as shown. Sew on the marked line. Trim ¼" from the stitched line. Press the dark green triangles toward the corners of the rectangles. Repeat on the opposite corner of another yellow and purple rectangle to make mirror-image units.

Make 1 of each.

6. Sew the yellow and purple units from step 5 together as shown. Press the seam allowances toward the yellow units.

Make 1 of each.

7. Sew each dark green triangle to a yellow triangle. Press the seam allowances toward the dark green triangles. Repeat with the light green triangles and the remaining yellow triangles. Press the seam allowances toward the yellow triangles.

Make 2 of each.

8. Sew one of each of the units from step 7 and a yellow rectangle together as shown.

Make 1 of each.

9. Sew the units created in steps 4, 6, and 8 together as shown.

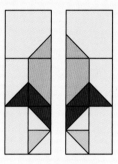

Make 1 of each.

10. Sew the units created in step 9 to each side of the unit created in step 3 as shown.

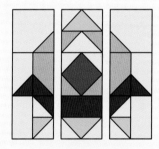

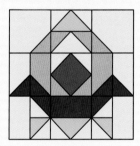

11. Repeat steps 1–10 to make a total of nine blocks.

About the Author

This is Terry's sixth quilting book, and she has many more ideas than time. She loves to lecture and teach classes, and hopes eventually to translate more of her quilting ideas into books. Terry is also the author of *Variations on a Theme: Quilts with Easy Options*.